# HORSEBACK RIDING

## by Flora Golden

Illustrated with photographs

**WOMEN IN SPORTS**

**Harvey House,** Publishers

New York, New York

The author gratefully acknowledges the assistance of Denise Boudrot, Sue Sally Jones, Helen Crabtree, Hilda Gurney and Michele McEvoy, especially for the use of personal photographs.
Additional photographs were supplied by Ed Lawrence, Golden Gate Park, Barbara McNight (polo photos).

*Women in Sports: Horseback Riding.*
*1. Horses. 2. Horsemanship — biography (collective).*
*798.23 (B)*

Library of Congress Catalogue Card Number 77-86361
Manufactured in the United States of America
ISBN 0-8178-5837-7

Published in Canada by Fitzhenry & Whiteside, Ltd., Toronto.

Harvey House, Publishers
20 Waterside Plaza
New York, New York 10010

*Dedicated to*
*Karen, Elizabeth and Marina*

# CONTENTS

In 1836, an American Magazine *article illustrated the
positions in riding for women — notice it is only side-
saddle. The article stated that women* "will learn to ride
chiefly for health ... and will not imitate the ladies of
Europe, by mixing in the race or in hunting."

# ONE Introduction

When Eleonara Sears galloped her horse onto a New York polo field in 1912, people were shocked. Instead of the traditional long riding skirt, she was dressed in breeches! She sat astride her horse — one leg on either side — when proper ladies only rode side-saddle. She was one of the growing number of American women who wanted to compete in horseback riding sports.

But ever since horseback riding became a sport in the early part of the nineteenth century, men have dominated the field. Before that time horses were used mostly for transportation or for work. There were few rules connected to riding.

By the year 1800, riding schools were established. People took lessons to improve their skills. Horseback riding contests were included in agricultural fairs; contestants being judged on their speed and the style of their riding.

Eventually horse shows grew up and were held separately from fairs. The rules became more complicated and judges were needed to enforce them. There were many different kinds of contests with jumping over obstacles one of the more popular ones.

In Europe, the earliest recorded show jumping contest was held in 1866 in Paris, France. By 1875 show jumping had reached England with special 'leaping' classes for ladies who jumped side-saddle.

The most important team jumping competition at England's International Horse Show was between Nations Cup Teams. Each team represented a country. The winners received a gold cup presented by the King of England.

Until 1945, these teams consisted of three men, all army officers, when Pat Smythe joined the team and became one of the first English women to gain international recognition as a show jumper. Her many honors included winning the European Women's Championship four times.

Pat proved that it wasn't necessary to be wealthy to be an international show jumper. Her first horse had been bred from a mare which pulled a milk wagon in an English village where she lived. The expensive horses she rode in international competitions were loaned by wealthy fans of the sport.

Pat Smythe went on to be the first woman to represent her country in show jumping in the Olympics when, in 1956, she competed for England in the Stockholm Games.

In America the most important equestrian teams were composed of cavalrymen (soldiers on horseback). In 1948 the cavalry broke up and, in 1949, the United States Equestrian Team Incorporated (USET Inc.) was created. This organization would select and finance equestrian teams to represent America in foreign countries.

The first team organized by the USET consisted of two men and two women. But the women, Carol Durand and Norma Mathews, weren't allowed to ride in the 1952 Olympic Games since rules barred women from competing in the equestrian events. Two men were chosen to replace them and the women had to watch from the sidelines.

By the 1956 Olympics, the rules had been changed to include women in the equestrian events. In 1962 Kathy Kusner, holder of the women's high jump record, joined the Pan American and the Olympic Teams. Kathy was the first woman to be selected for these honors by the USET in ten years. Kathy helped both teams win gold medals. She also scored the highest of any woman rider in the 1964 Olympics. But this wasn't enough for Kathy. She wanted to become a jockey too. Before 1967 no woman had been licensed to ride on a thoroughbred race track.

Kathy applied to the Maryland Racing Commission for a license but was turned down with the explanation that they didn't license amateur riders. (Kathy had remained an amateur since only amateurs could compete in the Olympic Games.)

Learning the Commission had previously licensed men who were amateurs, Kathy believed that the Commission was discriminating against her solely because she was a woman. Kathy and the Maryland Racing Commission went to court and a year-long battle followed. Finally the Commission's ruling was overturned on the basis of sex discrimination. On October 22, 1968, Kathy Kusner became the first woman to be granted a jockey's license.

A broken leg kept Kathy from riding her first scheduled race. But Dianne Crump, a shy exercise groom with a new jockey's license, rode in it. Although she finished tenth in the race, she went on to become the first woman to ride in the world famous Kentucky Derby.

Like Dianne Crump, other women jockeys were building careers. Barbara Jo Rubin, the first woman to win a race against men, and Robyn Smith, a Hollywood starlet turned jockey, were two who made racing news. Soon many women jockeys were competing in major tracks across the country.

Women faced discrimination in cross country jumping as well as horse racing. This rugged sport requires the horse and rider to jump natural obstacles — such as wagons and log piles — set in twenty-five miles of countryside.

The argument against women competing was if a woman should be thrown and injured, she wouldn't be strong enough to remount and finish the course as team members must. But since Vivian Goodall broke into the sport in 1953 in England, this male-oriented argument has been proven false many times. Lana Dupont (who was the first woman to compete in cross country in the Olympics) fell twice in mid-course. Remounting, she finished first in the 1964 Tokyo Olympics.

But a twenty-year-old American, Caroline Trevanus, provided the best example of a woman's determination in this sport. Competing in the 1974 World's Championship in England, she knew that her horse, Cajun, had misjudged the height of a rail jump. Horse and rider crashed into the jump and fell. Struggling to get up, Cajun rolled on top of Caroline. Despite a broken collar bone and several broken ribs, Caroline managed to remount and finished twenty-ninth out of fifty-nine entries. Her remarkable courage showed the experts that women can compete as well as men in cross country jumping.

Now there are growing opportunities for women in horseback riding sports of all kinds. Polo, horse racing and the Olympic Games are including more women than ever before. Equestrian sports are one of the few sports where men and women compete against each other and women frequently win.

# TYPES OF COMPETITION

One can horseback ride simply for personal pleasure or for the thrill of competition. In either case the possibilities are numerous.

Saddle seat equitation is performed with an American Saddle horse. This is no ordinary horse, but the most elegant of the show horses. He is bred for his shining coat, long neck and lively manner, and moves with such extraordinary grace that he has often been referred to as "the peacock of the show ring."

The American Saddle horse also has the special ability to learn five *gaits* (forward movements), two more than other horse breeds. In addition to the walk, trot and the gallop, the American Saddle horse can learn a slow gait and a *rack*. The slow gait resembles a running walk, except the horse lifts his legs high. The rack is much faster with the horse's hooves striking the ground one at a time while he carries the rider smoothly and swiftly forward.

Saddle seat equestrians spend many hours learning to make their high-spirited mounts perform at their best. The goal of most riders is to exhibit their horses in a show ring in either the three- or five-gaited classes.

Polo is the oldest equestrian sport. It is played from horseback with mallets and a ball on a long grass field. At each end of the field are a pair of goal posts.

To start the game, two four-player teams line up in the center of the field. The action begins when one of the three umpires rolls the ball between the lines.

The riders then try to strike the ball with their mallets as they gallop down the field. Their aim is to drive the ball swiftly over the grass and through the opposing team's goal posts for a goal. The team with the most goals wins.

The game is divided into six periods or *chukkers* of seven-and-a-half minutes each. Each chukker is packed with such fast action, the ponies are exhausted at the end. Polo players generally own several ponies so, between the chukkers, they change mounts.

Called ponies, the mounts used for polo are actually horses. In the olden days, the horses had to be small, but today there is no height limit.

15

A thoroughbred horse race begins at the instant the electrically operated starting gate opens. The horses, with jockeys clinging to their backs, bolt out and gallop around a flat oval track. The track is a mile to a mile-and-a-half in length.

A special camera photographs the horses as they cross the finish line. If there is disagreement as to who placed first, second, third and fourth, the camera has recorded the truth. The official results of the race are not announced until the film has been developed.

From his narrow nose to his long flowing tail, the thoroughbred has been bred for speed. He can gallop up to forty miles-per-hour. The jockeys are small and light so that their weight does not slow down the horse.

16

In dressage, the rider must guide her horse through many intricate movements. She controls the horse by using her hands, legs and body weights so subtly that the signals cannot be noticed by an observer. During the training, she also works to improve the physical condition and natural gaits of her horse.

The eight levels in competitive dressage are: Training, First, Second, Third and Fourth Levels, Prix St. Georges, Intermediate and Grand Prix. The Grand Prix is the one required at the Olympic Games.

Each level demands more difficult movements from the horse and rider. The pair progresses from one to the next by taking tests in an arena before judges. During the tests they are scored on such maneuvers as how smoothly they switch from a trot to a canter or how well they perform the *piaffer* (trotting-in-place).

Jumping can be the most exciting event for the spectator. Preliminary, Intermediate and Open are only some of the jumping levels. The most difficult jumps on the longest courses with the most prize money at stake are reserved for the highest level of all, the Grand Prix.

Most competitions require the horse and rider to jump a set number of obstacles in a certain order. The pair tries to complete the course as quickly as possible without any mistakes or faults.

Faults are made in a variety of ways. A rider, for example, may be faulted when his jumping horse's hooves brush a fence or when his horse refuses to jump altogether. In the end the faults are added up and the rider who has finished the course in the shortest time with the least number of faults wins.

Due to the determination of some outstanding women equestrians, professional polo, dressage, jumping, horse racing and saddle seat equitation have become increasingly open to women. Once women were primarily spectators in these equestrian sports. Today they not only compete, but win gold medals as well.

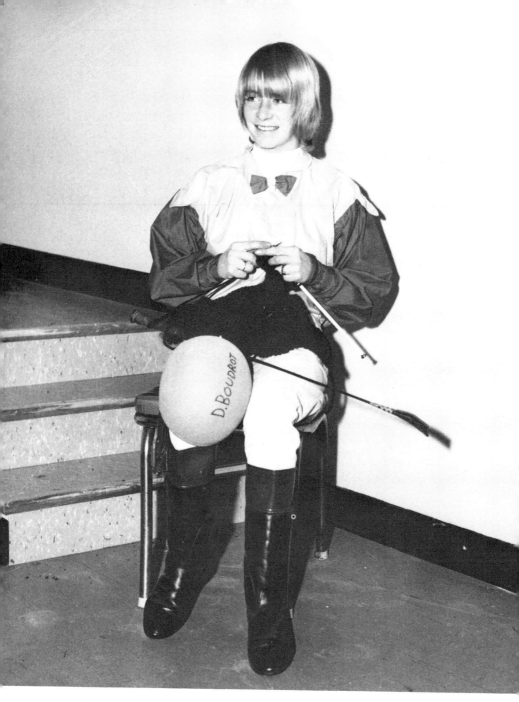

*Dressed in her racing silks, Denise Boudrot often knits or watches T.V. between races. She can have as many as five mounts in an afternoon.*

# TWO Denise Boudrot

When Denise was five years old, her father playfully swung her onto a pinto horse as it grazed in a field. He turned to speak to a friend and the horse suddenly bolted. It galloped toward a water trough far across the field while Denise hugged its sides with her legs and clung to its mane. Her father watched helplessly.

When the horse reached the water trough it stopped to drink. Denise glanced back at her pale and shaken father. "Do it again! Do it again!" she cried.

Denise did do it again, many times. In fact, since then she has spent much of her life on galloping horses.

When she was a high school sophomore, she decided she wanted to be a jockey. She had read exciting articles about women jockeys in magazines and newspapers. "Over my dead body!" her father had replied. "You'll never go to the track."

Then, the summer after her high school graduation, Denise was struck by a car as she crossed a street. Her leg was broken. "I just laid around recuperating. I guess my father felt sorry for me," she recalled, "because one day he said, 'I thought you were going to be a jockey.' He actually reminded me."

Denise later discovered that her father hadn't really been opposed to the idea. He had been afraid that if he had encouraged her too early, she'd have quit high school to pursue her career.

Denise's interest in horses had increased greatly when she was eleven and her older brother David gave her a horse. He was called Sachem, an old American Indian name meaning "Wise Old Chief." Denise cantered Sachem through the woods and the sand pits behind their home. Most of all, she loved to ride him in horse shows as a member of the 4-H Pacesetters in Burlington, Massachusetts, where she lived.

In those days, she was known as "Sam." She got the nickname from her brother, after her father had let a barber clip her hair short as a boy's. Later, even though her mother curled her hair every night, the nickname stuck.

At seventeen, Denise visited a track for the first time to help care for a friend's thoroughbred. She had never before seen anything as exciting as a horse race. Glued to her seat, eyes fixed on the jockeys crouched low in their saddles, she kept mumbling, "I'll never do that. I'll never do that." Yet two years later, in 1972, she got her jockey's license.

During those two years, Denise had begun her career by grooming race horses. At Lincoln Downs Racetrack in Massachusetts she also led them onto the track while riding an ordinary horse.

While at Lincoln Downs she found out Maurice Bresnahan, a prominent horse trainer, was looking for a girl to exercise horses at his farm, Holly Hill, in South Carolina. Denise got the job and a three-year contract.

At Holly Hill, Denise learned how to leave a starting gate and to control a horse on the track. She accomplished in three short months what it took other riders a couple of years to do.

By the end of her second year with Bresnahan, Denise was assigned to her first race at Rockingham Park in New Hampshire. She rode the horse, O.B.'s Viking, and placed a disappointing sixth.

*A hopeful apprentice jockey, Denise awaits her first race aboard O.B.'s Viking at Rockingham Park. Her sixth place showing was a discouraging one.*

*Denise made her own history at Suffolk Downs with both her first and hundredth wins there.*

Not easily discouraged, she had her first taste of victory on Misty Colfax at Suffolk Downs, Boston three months later. Before she even left the winner's circle, her mind began to spin with thoughts of winning her next race.

Denise has won 454 races to date. She has brought in as many as five winners in one afternoon. In 1974, she had 94 winners in 90 days, becoming the first woman apprentice jockey to be top-ranked at a major track.

An apprentice jockey is a newcomer to horse racing. Because he is less experienced than a regular jockey, his mount is allowed to carry five pounds less weight than the other mounts in the race. This is an advantage because the less weight a horse carries, the faster it is likely to go. An apprentice or a *bug*, as he is sometimes called, loses this weight advantage one year after he wins his fifth race.

With her record, Denise is the talk of thoroughbred racing. Sports fans across the country have watched her interviewed on television and have read in national magazines about the fantastic woman jockey who earns between $45,000 and $75,000 a year.

Today it's not uncommon for women to race thoroughbreds. Yet it wasn't so very long ago that women jockeys were unheard of. Not until the late 1960's did women begin to invade this sport traditionally reserved for men. Penny Ann Early, Robyn Smith and Diane Crump were a few of the women jockeys who fought their way into a field that definitely didn't want them. Their persistent efforts made it easier for other women to follow in their footsteps.

Still, Denise had problems as a female jockey, particularly in the early part of her career. She also had to confront hostile fans and uncooperative trainers.

"Go home and have babies. You should be doing dishes," the fans would shout from the grandstand.

The trainers gave many excuses to keep her from securing mounts. Some of the excuses were outrageous. "They'd say anything from 'My wife will be mad at me if I let you ride,' to 'Girls aren't strong enough to handle horses,'" Denise recalls.

But Denise managed to pick up a few mounts anyway. "The more I won, the less the trainers could give me the same old excuses," she says.

In fact the more she won, the more they wanted her to ride and the better mounts she got. And riding the fastest horses is the only road to success in this competitive sport.

What's it like to be a woman jockey? Up at sunrise, Denise leaves her apartment, which she shares with a Chihuahua and a German Shepherd. She arrives at the track at 6 a.m. for the morning workout. Then she chats with trainers and lines up future mounts.

At 10 she breaks for breakfast. "I'm currently into spaghetti," she says. Then she naps until 2 p.m. when it's time to climb into her jockey silks.

Denise usually has between three and five mounts an afternoon. Between races she watched the films of her previous race on closed circuit television in the jockeys' room, usually rooting loudly for herself. Then she switches to the soap operas to relax.

Denise heads home about 5 p.m. There she enjoys television, reads, or works on art projects. Sometimes she goes out to dinner with a friend. Always in bed between 8 and 9 p.m., she needs plenty of rest for the physically demanding job of racing the next day.

It takes both strength and courage to race thoroughbreds. It also takes thought and Denise is an excellent jockey because she analyzes the habits of her mounts. By the second time out, she has learned whether they run best close to the rail or on the outside. She also knows if they will be more likely to win by starting the race out in front of the others or by galloping up from behind.

The more she learns about her mount, the better she can respond to whatever happens during the race. "When you are on a horse's back your reflexes are super-quick. When he moves you react. You're

*As much physical energy is used in the maintenance of horse and equipment as in the actual racing.*

constantly making split-second decisions," Denise says. These decisions are necessary not only for winning, but for preventing accidents. Still, Denise has had her share of the latter.

In one race, another horse clipped the heels of her mount. Her mount went down and Denise went with him, injuring her back. Another time, she was racing a horse that hit the outside rail. It fell and landed in a ditch. Denise landed in the hospital with a broken leg. In yet another race, she was cut off from the rail position by a loose horse that had unseated its rider earlier. She once lost her stirrups and had to finish the race gripping

27

*After a grueling race, mud-covered Denise proves that being a jockey is not always glamorous.*

the horse with her legs, bareback-style. These incidents were frightening, but neither one resulted in injury.

All jockeys live with danger. But they can't afford to dwell on it if they want to be successful. Denise says, "If you're always thinking about what can happen — and so many things do happen — you'll constantly be scared. And you can't ride scared. It's impossible. You won't be a good rider."

The rugged nature of the sport has certainly not discouraged women from participating. Today there are many women jockeys riding in major tracks across the country.

Denise advises girls who are interested in becoming jockeys to get a job at a racehorse farm where instruction is available. "They need to get lots of experience," she says. "I was getting on seven, eight or nine horses a day. I broke out of the starting gate over two hundred times before I rode my first race."

Denise's future plans include eventually moving to her farm in South Carolina which she bought with her prize money. When she decides to retire from riding, she will concentrate on breeding thoroughbreds and training them there.

Until then, however, Denise has a long and exciting career ahead. "The key to success in this business," Denise says, "is to like what you are doing, whether you're male or female."

*A dedicated horsewoman, Michele McEvoy lovingly strokes a possible future champion at Rock Bottom Farms.*

# THREE — Michele McEvoy

In the center training ring at Rock Bottom Farms, Michele McEvoy gallops on horseback toward a high wooden jump. As the horse soars, Michele rises in the saddle. She feels the wind in her hair and on her cheeks, and for an exhilarating moment, she is flying. Then the horse's hooves strike the earth and horse and rider are off again, gathering speed for the next jump.

Michele first learned to ride at Windmill Stables near her home in Summit, New Jersey. From the beginning, she desperately wanted her own horse, but her parents refused to buy her one. They didn't realize how serious their nine-year-old daughter was about horseback riding.

A close family friend, Malcolm McLean, used to say to Michele, "Don't worry, you'll get that horse you want. I'll see to it."

"I would cry a lot when he told me that," Michele recalls, "because I knew that Mr. McLean liked to joke and I thought that he was teasing me."

Then on Christmas Eve the phone rang at the McEvoy's home. It was Mr. McLean for Michele. Clutching the phone receiver, Michele could hardly believe what she heard. Mr. McLean told her that he had bought her a horse named Red.

Michele rode Red before school, after school and on weekends too. Michele's father decided that if he wanted to see his daughter at all, he'd better take up riding. From then on, Michele and her father spent many happy Saturdays cantering their horses along the trails. Soon Mr. McEvoy grew as enthusiastic about the sport as his daughter. Over several years he bought and sold thirty-six horses and ponies for them both. One pony, named Dandelion, had a mean disposition and had thrown Michele off with such force that she broke both arms.

But trail riding wasn't enough for Michele. She loved the wonderful, free feeling that she got from jumping, and when she was fourteen, she began to work with Carl Knee at his Rock Bottom Farms in Millbrook, New York. Knee had an excellent reputation for coaching riding champions and Michele soon jumped her horses over big and small, wide and narrow obstacles. While Carl enthusiastically encouraged her, as a good coach he also pointed out her mistakes.

Michele began to enter horse shows, collecting trophies and ribbons at an astonishing rate. At seventeen, she was the only rider to win the Horse of the Year Award in the Junior Hunter and Junior Jumper Division.

Michele had now competed in all jumping contests, except the most challenging, the Grand Prix. In this class the jumps are extremely difficult — up to six and a half feet high and sixteen feet wide. At certain points the horse and rider must leap across water. Although Michele was experienced enough for Grand Prix classes, she didn't own a horse to work with for that purpose. She wanted to buy such a jumper, but, so far, she couldn't find exactly the right horse.

While looking, Michele heard that the prize-winning Grand Prix champion, Sundancer, was for sale in Canada. Carl and Michele flew there at once.

*With this winning style, Michele rides to her first international competition victory in Rome, 1974.*

Sundancer looked like a winner. A beautiful chestnut thoroughbred, he had fine bone structure, long legs and a glossy coat.

The first time Sundancer and Michele tried a jump together, Michele knew that Sundancer suited her perfectly. She noticed that he didn't pull on the reins like other horses. Michele, only 4 feet 11 inches tall, didn't want a horse strong enough to overpower her. Yet Sundancer was a splendid jumper, sailing over even the highest obstacles with seemingly little effort.

After the McEvoys bought Sundancer, he was sent to Rock Bottom Farms. There, Michele and her horse practiced for many hours together. She had with Sundancer a special kind of communication that she had never known with any other horse. Sundancer seemed to anticipate what she wanted him to do and with his Grand Prix experience, the horse was able to teach Michele quite a bit. They worked beautifully together, developing into a magnificent team.

At last Michele and Sundancer were ready to enter Grand Prix classes. They competed in both the United States and Europe, thrilling crowds wherever they went. The spectators loved to watch the petite girl guide the huge thoroughbred over breathtaking jumps.

In 1974, when Michele was twenty, she placed second in the Ladies World Championship at La Baule, France. In the same year, she became the leading rider at the Rome International Horse Show in Rome, Italy.

Michele was delighted to win her first international competition. This made her an important figure in show-

*Aboard Sundancer, the horse "made for me," Michele became the leading rider at the Rome International Horse Show in 1974.*

jumping circles. It also increased her chances to be selected for the 1976 Olympic Team.

But before becoming an Olympic team member, she first had to be chosen for the Pan American team. The Pan American competition is held a year before the Olympic Games.

There are five Pan American team tryouts for jumpers. These are Grand Prix contests which are held in Ohio, New York and other states. A rider must participate in three of these events in order to be eligible for the team.

Michele and Sundancer entered four. Winning two firsts, a second, a third and many other ribbons, they had the best record of any of the horses and riders.

Yet they were not chosen for the team. Michele, as well as show-jumping experts were terribly disappointed. They didn't understand why the selection committee had excluded Michele and Sundancer.

Michele believed that her reputation as a one-horse rider may have damaged her chances. The committee reasoned that she didn't have enough Grand Prix experience to be successful on another horse if Sundancer were injured and couldn't jump.

Michele's weight was still another problem. At 115 pounds, she was light for a Grand Prix competitor. All horses are required to carry 165 pounds. The difference between the rider's weight and the 165 pounds is made up in dead weight or lead bars which are slipped into the horse's saddle pad. Although dead weight is the most difficult kind for the horse to carry, Sundancer jumped beautifully with Michele's 115 pounds and the extra fifty pounds. But if Sundancer would not be available, would another horse be able to do as well?

It was also rumored that women jumpers are less likely than men to be selected for both the Pan American and Olympic teams. Women aren't as strong as men, and this was considered a disadvantage. Plus, the few women who had been chosen as team members in the past gave disappointing performances. Therefore, the selection committee was less likely to take a chance on more women, no matter how promising they appeared. In spite of her disappointment, Michele and Sundancer continued to compete. Then in 1976, at the

Chagrin Valley Horse Show in Ohio, Sundancer bumped his leg as he crossed a jump. The next morning the leg was swollen and infected. The infection spread and the horse was rushed to the top veterinarian experts at the University of Pennsylvania's Equine Center. In spite of their efforts to save him, he grew steadily worse. Finally, Sundancer had to be destroyed.

"Every competitive rider has one horse in his career made for him," Michele says. "Sundancer was made for me. When he died, I felt as though I had lost a very close friend."

There may never be another Sundancer, but Michele continues to work successfully. Presently, she owns two promising Grand Prix jumpers, Night Murmur and Semi-Pro. She takes them on the jumping circuit of horse shows located in various Eastern cities. From February to November, a special group of riders, their horses in vans, travels caravan-style from show from show. Michele drives with them in company of her two Whippets, Rosie and Wilman.

Most horse shows have two arenas, with different contests happening in each. When she rides, Michele spends most of the day rushing back and forth between them.

Besides jumping Semi-Pro and Night Murmur, she shows many young horses which she and Carl both own and train. She hopes that people will admire and buy them. By selling these horses, Michele pays for her own and her thoroughbred's expenses.

*An inseparable team, Michele and Sundancer entered the Pan American Team tryouts in 1975.*
*With astoundingly successful jumps, the team racked up the best record of any horse and rider but failed to be chosen for the team. Note lead weights on Sundancer.*

Michele's plans include competing in Europe and possibly in the next Olympic Games. Her hopes for the future Olympics rest with Semi-Pro, her favorite jumper. By that time, she knows she will have enough Grand Prix experience for the selection committee's satisfaction.

With Michele's talent, there is an excellent chance she will be chosen for the United States Equestrian Team in the 1980 Olympic Games.

# FOUR Hilda Gurney

Many young horseback riders dream of riding in the Olympic Games. This is the story of Hilda Gurney, who not only shared that dream, but made it come true.

Hilda lived with her parents and her four older brothers and sisters. Their home was a beautiful, old Spanish-style house set high atop a hill in Woodland Hills, California.

Below their house stretched acres of squash fields which were owned by the old-time movie star Mae West. Hilda's brothers and sisters liked to ride Pete, the old white horse that plowed the fields.

One day, they boosted Hilda up onto Pete. For the three-year old girl, it seemed like miles down to the ground. Yet the moment she sat on Pete's broad back, her interest in horses blossomed.

Hilda's parents didn't approve of their youngest daughter's enthusiasm for horses and preferred that Hilda spend her time in other ways.

For eight years Hilda took ballet lessons, studied the French horn and the piano. But tucked away in her mind, was her enormous desire to ride.

When Hilda was nine she had earned enough money babysitting to afford ten riding lessons. When her money ran out, she had to stop since her parents didn't want her to borrow her friends' horses. Deciding the only

*Hilda Gurney patiently works Keen through his intricate dressage movements at Hilda's ring next to her home in Woodland Hills, California.*

way to ride again was to own a horse, she began to save her money again. At fourteen she had enough to buy Grandy, a thoroughbred.

She had owned him only a year when Grandy tripped over a rock one day, broke his leg, and had to be destroyed. This taught Hilda a sad lesson about how fragile horses can be.

At seventeen, she began to work at Onondarka Stables near her home. She broke and trained horses for four years while she went to college for her teaching degree.

In 1969, when she was twenty-five, Hilda entered the United States National Championship at Pebble Beach, California. Hilda first competed in jumping and then switched to combined training for the States National Championship. In this event, the same horse and rider compete in three separate tests: dressage (lower levels), cross-country (jumping obstacles in an outdoor course) and stadium (jumping high obstacles in an enclosed arena).

The finest riders from the United States and foreign countries gathered for this important event so Hilda found herself competing against all of the members of the United States Olympic Team. She was the only woman, the only Californian, and the only person not connected with an Olympic Team to be in the show.

To her delight, Hilda won the combined training event. This was her first major victory in a national competition. She was very encouraged and began to think seriously about the Olympic Games. Perhaps she would be ready to ride in them sooner than she had expected.

Although Hilda had been successful in combined training, she turned her interest toward dressage. It was easier on the horses.

Hilda learned advanced dressage from the famous Dressage Institute in New York State. The following summer, the institute's instructors came to California to teach Hilda and some friends.

Before that, while attending the 1968 Olympic Games in Mexico City, Hilda had paid careful attention to the type of dressage horse used there. She noticed the Russians and the Germans (who had won first and second place) rode large, powerful animals.

When Hilda returned home, she decided to buy a horse to train for dressage only. She searched breeding farms, and looked at many privately-owned horses for sale.

At a thoroughbred farm in Riverside, California, she found Keen. A huge three-year old, he was exactly the sort of horse that the Russians and the Germans had ridden in Mexico. Despite his size he moved gracefully. He also had a fine temperament.

The farm manager said that Keen had been a failure at the racetrack. He could hardly leave the starting gate without stumbling. Undiscouraged, Hilda wanted to buy Keen anyway. But he wasn't for sale because the owners were going to trade him for a heifer they needed.

Hilda went home but she didn't forget Keen. She called the farm regularly to ask how the trade was coming. Several months later she was told the trade had fallen through. If she wanted Keen, she could have him.

Hilda, terribly excited, bought Keen at once and

took him home. Then she began the slow, patient work of dressage training in the dirt ring beside her house. Hilda started by teaching Keen to move in a relaxed but lively manner. She improved his walk, trot and canter by establishing a regular rhythm.

Eventually Keen was ready to learn more complicated movements, such as leg yielding. Here the horse crosses one hind leg over the other hind leg and one front leg over the other one. This propels him forward and sideways at the same time.

After Hilda and Keen had completed the seven levels of dressage training, they were ready to tackle the eighth — and the hardest. It includes such difficult maneuvers as the *pirouette* (circling in place at a walk and a canter), *piaffer* (trot in place) and the *passage* (slow motion trot).

Dressage riding involves communication between the horse and the rider and therefore most horses take six years to accomplish all eight levels. Keen, who is very talented, learned in only three and a half.

"Basically, you and the horse are partners in a ballet together," Hilda says. "When you are on his back you tell him every muscle to move."

Many dressage experts were critical of Keen. They thought that he was too large to perform the intricate dressage maneuvers. But Hilda had confidence in Keen. She worked him five days a week for several years and her determination paid off. Hilda was terribly proud when Keen won Horse of the Year for California in the

*Left, Hilda and Keen relax after a good schooling session. Right, in 1969, Hilda rode Flag's Elf and won the gold medal in the Open Division of the 12th Annual Pebble Beach Three Day Event.*

First and Second Level in 1970. When Keen was selected as Horse Of The Year for the United States at the International Level, Hilda was prouder still.

Hilda continued to ride Keen in the most important contests in the country and won many top awards. In 1975 they competed in the tryouts for the Pan American Team whose games are held every four years in either North or South America.

Hilda, wanting to be part of this prestigious team, knew that only the most talented riders are chosen.

45

Seven hard-to-please judges select only the top three riders out of many.

In the tryouts, Hilda and Keen placed second and third in two separate contests and this qualified them for the team.

When the Pan American Games were held the same year in Mexico City, Hilda and Keen were triumphant there too. Winning a silver medal, they helped their team earn two gold ones as well.

Being chosen for the Olympic Team (a more difficult team to make than the Pan American) is the highest honor an American equestrian can achieve. So, when the Olympic screening trials were held in Gladstone, New Jersey, Hilda and Keen were there competing against twenty-two of America's finest dressage champions for three regular and one alternate place.

Once again Hilda and Keen were successful. Their excellent performance earned them a spot on the team and Hilda was elated. She and Keen would go to Montreal, Canada for the 1976 Olympic Games.

Extending over a three day period, the Olympic dressage competition consists of two tests, the Grand Prix and the Grand Prix Special. The Grand Prix requires all the difficult movements in the eighth level, and only the horses and riders who place in the top twelve can ride in the Grand Prix Special where the same maneuvers are performed.

Before her test, Hilda put on her high top hat. She slipped into her black coat with the long tails, her white britches and her shiny boots — the dressage uniform.

The grandstands were jammed with people. They had flocked from all over the world to witness this spectacular event which is held only once every four years. Brightly-colored flags fluttered overhead and a band played loudly as Hilda moved Keen onto the field.

To keep herself calm, Hilda pretended she was riding in a less important competition than the Olympic Games. Most of the other contestants had been to the Olympics before, gaining valuable experience Hilda and Keen didn't have. Hilda worried Keen wouldn't do well against the European horses. He had been successful in American competitions, but the European dressage horses are the best in the world.

As Hilda put Keen through his paces, she hoped they would place in the top twelve. The only American to succeed in doing this since the United States Cavalry Team rode in the Olympics many years ago was Trish Galvin, in the 1960 Rome Olympics.

To Hilda's amazement, she and Keen placed fourth the first day and tenth the second. They didn't earn an individual medal, but their team won a bronze one.

Although Hilda wasn't first in the Olympic Games, she was first in other important ways: the first American and the first woman to train a horse to compete in the Olympics. She was also the first dressage rider who didn't spend a lot of money. (Usually people who want to compete at the Olympic level will go to Europe and buy an expensive, well-trained dressage horse. The person will live there for several years, studying dressage full-time under an excellent instructor).

*Dressed in the required top hat and tails, Hilda rode Keen in the 1976 Olympic Games in Montreal, Canada. She was the first woman, as well as American, to train an Olympic horse.*

Today, Hilda is an elementary school teacher. She cannot devote all of her time to training horses and her dressage activities have to fit into her busy teaching schedule.

But Hilda Gurney is a good example for many. Her story proves to girls and boys who ride that it is not necessary to own an expensive horse and to live in Europe to compete in the Olympic Games as a dressage rider.

Hilda explains it this way. Those children can now say, "Here is an American girl who trained her own horse. If she can make the United States Equestrian Team, then maybe I can too."

# FIVE Sue Sally Jones

Sue Sally Jones walked her horse off the Will Rogers Polo Field. "I'll never make a decent polo player," she thought.

Only an hour before Sue Sally had been wildly happy. Duke Coulter, who ran the Will Rogers Polo Team, had invited her to join them for a game when they needed a last minute replacement.

Sue Sally had dreamt about playing polo with this team since she was a little girl. Although she was a pretty skillful player, she was only fourteen and had not expected to compete in their matches. After all, this experienced group of men had never included a girl before.

But now, by a stroke of luck, she had her chance. Tucking her yellow braids beneath her helmet, she grabbed her mallet. Then, climbing onto her horse, she trotted out on the field where the others were waiting.

50

*A successful athlete and businesswoman today, Sue Sally Jones finds time to play polo as well as run the Carmel Valley Riding Center singlehandedly.*

The match got off to a fast start. Sue Sally charged into the middle of the action and just as she had maneuvered close enough to whack the ball, she heard someone call her name. Sue Sally glanced up to see Duke, the team captain, galloping toward her. When he was close enough, he began to tell her exactly how to play. From then on Duke stuck close to Sue Sally with a steady stream of instructions.

Sue Sally was embarrassed. She thought that she must be making terrible mistakes — why else was Duke shouting corrections at her? She felt that the other players must be annoyed at her for interfering with their game so when the match was over, she quickly packed her gear and left the field without a word to anyone.

The following Sunday, even though a match was scheduled, Sue Sally didn't appear at the Will Rogers Polo Grounds. Normally Sue Sally never missed a match.

On Monday, Duke called her on the phone. "Where were you?" he barked.

"I thought that all of your shouting meant that I wasn't any good. I was embarrassed to show up."

"You wanna play polo?"

"Yes."

"Then be here next Sunday."

When Sue Sally saw Duke he explained that he had meant for his instructions to help her, not to criticize her. He had been very impressed by her ability on the field, and told her that she was far too good to watch from the sidelines. Then he asked her if she would follow a training program that he and his polo-playing friend, C.D. LeBlanc, had planned to organize for her.

Would she ever! And so Sue Sally's career as a polo player was launched.

Sue Sally loved polo since she was five years old. She would ride her pony to the polo grounds near her home in Pacific Palisades, California to watch the games. Excited by the helmeted players who swung their mallets from galloping horses, she could hardly sit still in her saddle.

As she grew older, she spent all of her spare time at the polo grounds retrieving stray balls and walking over-heated horses for the Will Rogers Polo Team. She would do anything to be part of the game.

*On the polo grounds at age eleven, Sue Sally already knew what she wanted — as her mother's yellowed paper still shows.*

The team members responded to Sue Sally's interest by teaching her polo and she was an enthusiastic student. For months after school until the sun sank behind the deserted polo field, she'd practice driving the ball over the grass toward the goal posts.

When she was twelve years old, Sue Sally gave serious thought to her future. "I'm going to be a bronc rider or a polo player," she told her mother one day. Mrs. Jones wondered if Sue Sally really was determined enough to become either. Scribbling her daughter's words down on a piece of paper, she told Sue Sally to sign her name at the bottom. Then she tucked the paper into her pocket.

At fifteen, after following Duke Coulter's and C.D. LeBlanc's training program, she was skillful enough to play with the experts at the Will Rogers Polo Grounds. Sue Sally quickly became a crowd favorite. People were fascinated by the blue-eyed blonde girl who could wallop the ball from a galloping horse as well as any man. They'd shout her name and applaud as she raced past.

By then Sue Sally owned two horses. She paid for their expenses by teaching riding and continued to give instruction through high school and college. Finally she earned enough money to buy herself a string of four polo ponies.

Although Sue Sally was happy playing polo, she had problems. Most polo clubs didn't want her. She was a fine enough player, but the fact was that they didn't want women. Although fans loved the teenager, many teams refused to play against a woman.

Sue Sally also wanted to play matches that were sanctioned by the United States Polo Association. These included the teams with the best players. Most of all she wanted to compete in the match for the Governor's Cup, but one had to belong to the association to qualify for these games and Sue Sally wasn't a member. In 1956, when she was sixteen, she had tried to join, but the polo association turned her down because they didn't accept women. Every year for seventeen years thereafter, Sue Sally applied for membership. Her application, though, was always rejected.

At twenty-three, Sue Sally married Alex Hale and they moved to Northern California. In Point Lobos, on the Monterey Peninsula, they bought an old house with enough land for horses. Starting with the two that she had kept, Sue Sally began to acquire more. Then she and Alex started a family with the birth of their first child.

The Monterey Peninsula, with its towering pine trees and ocean breezes, was an ideal place to live and to raise children. But Sue Sally wasn't happy there. It seemed the peninsula had everything — except polo.

Not the sort of person who sat around feeling sorry for herself, Sue Sally decided she would do something about it. She began by giving riding lessons. She was excellent at working with children and horses and soon her reputation spread. Her classes grew larger. It wasn't

*Sue Sally rides Maya in the August 1977 "Go Honey Tourney" in Santa Barbara.*

long before several of her students had learned to ride well enough for Sue Sally to give them helmets, knee pads and mallets. Finally she could begin to teach them polo.

Her first team was made up of teenage girls and later a few boys joined in. Some of the parents caught their children's enthusiasm and took up riding and soon there were enough people to form two adult teams.

Sue Sally then organized the first polo club on the Monterey Peninsula since World War II. She also began to plan informal polo tournaments.

Eventually, Sue Sally, Alex, their son, Brook, and two daughters, Storm and Dawn, moved a few miles away to Carmel Valley. They had rented a ranch house and a farm located at the end of a narrow bumpy road. Sunset, a third daughter was born on moving day. Another son, Trails, followed a year later.

On the farm was a huge barn and enough paddocks for the family's horses and boarders. But best of all there was enough room for a full-sized polo field.

When her new field was completed, Sue Sally invited polo clubs from all over California to play tournaments. Her warmth and hospitality attracted many polo players. The fact that these matches weren't sanctioned by the United States Polo Association didn't prevent the finest teams from competing there.

*Sue Sally's polo club, the first on Monterey Peninsula since World War II, attracted much competition from clubs all over California.*

A number of the men became friendly with Sue Sally. Admiring her skill and devotion to the sport, several took an interest in her membership fight with the United States Polo Association and decided to help her. They spoke to officials of the organization about this woman who had loved polo since childhood. They praised her ability and her contribution to the game and argued against the inequity of restricting membership to men.

Eventually the assocation relented. In 1972, Sue Sally and her team, the Carmel Valley Polo Club, were admitted. Sue Sally became the first woman member.

The United States Polo Assocation sanctioned many matches which are for members only. Sue Sally was no longer excluded from these. Now she could play more polo than ever before.

*At 23, Sue Sally was still nearly ten years away from being accepted into the all-male U.S. Polo Association.*

Today Sue Sally and Alex are divorced. Brook, their fourteen year old son, lives with his father. The other children, Dawn, Stormy, Trails and Sunset, remain with their mother in the ranch house.

In this bright sunny home, there is likely to be a cat or a dog curled up in every chair and a litter of newborn pups in the bathtub. There is even a chicken perched in a bird cage on a living room table.

Sue Sally's day begins at 4:30 a.m. when she rises for bookkeeping and housework. At 8 she exercises her first horse at the farm. She trains horses, teaches riding and polo plus two college classes in horsemanship.

Although polo has provided Sue Sally with a rich and satisfying life, she sometimes finds it difficult to be treated equally as a woman in a male-dominated sport.

It has been Sue Sally's experience that because she is a woman she can't cancel out on a match and expect to be included next time, although she notices a man often can. She must always play her best and offer no excuses if something goes wrong. Because she is on trial, she finds that it's her mediocre games which are remembered instead of her good ones. This damages her chances to participate in future games.

Rarely is she asked to be the team captain, the team member who dictates the plays. Since she can't be a leader, she must always rely on someone else's decisions.

Despite these difficulties, Sue Sally wouldn't have chosen another career. A talented teacher, she singlehandedly runs the Carmel Valley Riding Center. She has helped bring amateur and professional polo to hundreds of people on the Monterey Peninsula. As the first woman member in the United States Polo Association, she has pioneered the way for others to follow.

Several years ago, Sue Sally's mother handed her daughter a yellowed, crumpled piece of paper. "I'm going to be a bronc rider or a polo player," Sue Sally read. She smiled recalling her childhood vow. She certainly had made it come true.

# six Helen Crabtree

It is a hot summer day in Louisville, Kentucky and the horse show is about to begin. People, dressed in riding jackets and jodphurs (riding breeches), are hurrying about the show grounds. A few are on horseback.

In her red golf cart with the big brass horn in front, Helen Crabtree is driving back and forth between the show ring and the barn doing last minute errands. She is the coach of several girls who are showing their American Saddle horses this afternoon. She is the trainer of their horses as well.

Helen's students — "the Crabtree girls" — anxiously wait in the barn. Three of the girls are twelve, one thirteen and one fourteen. As show time approaches, they grow more and more jittery. They smooth their hair, straighten their bowler hats and adjust their brightly-colored flowers in their coat lapels. One girl is so nervous she mounts the wrong horse!

At last everyone is correctly mounted. As the girls walk their horses out of the barn, Helen steers her cart toward the white fence surrounding the ring to have a close view of the show.

She watches her students ride into the ring. Sitting perfectly balanced in their saddles, they have that easy control over their horses that marks expert equestrians.

"Canter, please, canter," comes the order over the loudspeaker.

As the horses pound by, Helen can't resist coaching from ringside. "Very nice. Very nice," she calls to one of her riders. To another she yells, "Be careful! You're too close to the horse in front!"

The Crabtree girls are performing well. They seem to be remembering all they have learned from Helen at Crabtree Farms, the family home near Simpsonville, Kentucky where Helen teaches girls — and an occasional boy — to ride and show their American Saddle horses. Helen's students are not casual riders. They have either competed in top horse shows across the country or plan to. During their school vacations, the students occupy special apartments tucked among the farm's lush green hills, board fences, dogwood and magnolia trees. They also board their horses at Crabtree Farms for Helen to train.

The girls' training begins at 10:00 a.m. when they meet Helen at the farm's indoor practice ring. If the class is large, ten for example, Helen divides it into two sections. While five mount up to ride, the others will watch. Later riders and observers change places. The five who are observing follow Helen to her glass-enclosed instruction booth in one corner of the ring. From there they have a perfect view of the riders on their high-stepping horses.

"Did you notice your horse cut the corner? Watch the next one because he'll do it again," Helen warns a rider through a microphone.

To the observers, Helen says, "Feel the tingle in your fingers as though you are holding the reins. Feel the pressure in your legs as though you are in the saddle." She believes the students can learn as much from watching others as they can from riding.

Helen teaches by helping the girls to observe and by correcting mistakes in the practice ring. She also teaches by explanation, as though they were in a classroom. While the riders sit quietly on their horses, Helen instructs them how to correctly place their feet in the stirrups and how to hold the reins. She also discusses the importance of keeping a proper distance between the horse in front and the one behind in a horse show.

Helen often tells her students, "Put yourself in the bridle. You have to think like a horse to do your best riding." She insists this is essential in order to prevent mistakes.

*A winning horse and rider combination trained by Helen Crabtree is a common occurrence in any ring. Here, at the far right, Helen is present at the awards ceremony.*

In a show ring, for example, a rider must keep her horse close to the rail. Most horses, however, try to cut across the corners, thereby shortening the distance they have to travel around the ring. Then they can return to the entrance gate sooner and leave the ring. A rider can prevent this by anticipating what the horse may do. Then she can pull in the reins and apply heel pressure as the corners approach.

A Crabtree girl becomes an expert equestrian by observing, by practicing and by learning about horse behavior. Once she has good control over her horse she is ready for the show ring.

Back at the horse show it is time for the judging. The riders, having been asked to line their horses up in the center of the ring, appear calm, but their hearts are beating rapidly. From her cart, Helen watches the judges mark their score cards.

At last the decision is announced over the loudspeaker. The winner is a Crabtree girl! Helen dashes into the ring to congratulate her. She poses for a photographer with the winning horse and the smiling rider, who is clutching a trophy.

Once again Helen has helped another student to victory. She can add one more gold disk engraved with the winner's name to her already crowded, favorite bracelet.

The secret to Helen's many coaching successes is in teaching her riders to be lively performers. They are never encouraged to ride cautiously simply to avoid making mistakes. Instead, they must push their horses to step higher with every stride or to gain more speed at the rack.

"Give it all you've got, even though you make an occasional mistake," advises Helen. "To be a Crabtree winner you've got to get everything out of that horse that it's got to give."

When it comes to teaching horses and riders, Helen gives everything she's got to give and her hard work has paid off. Her students include nineteen winners of both the American Horse Show Association Medal Finals and the National Horse Show's Good Hands, the most coveted awards for saddle seat competitions. In addition, Helen has turned no fewer than fifty-three horses into world champions.

Born on a farm in 1915, Helen Kitner loved to train animals even as a child. To her, a chicken had possibilities. Once, when one darted out on the stairs before her, Helen accidentally stepped on it and broke its leg. She made the chicken a splint, tamed it and taught it to do tricks.

From the time Helen had first climbed up on her father's working mules at the age of two, she desperately wanted to ride. "Anything with four legs was in dire danger when I was around," recalls Helen, who even rode pigs and cows.

She entered her first horse show at four. "Back then little girls didn't show horses. People would come from miles around to see the little Kitner girl ride," says Helen. "I was the only female youngster in the ring. I was competing against males and beating them. They might have resented me, but they had to respect me."

When Helen was eight, her father bought his daughters their first horse. Helen reluctantly shared Lady, a pretty little chestnut mare, with one of her two older sisters, Martha.

At twelve Helen became a full-fledged horse trainer. Since she had become the best rider in the country, people gave her their most difficult horses to work with.

After she was graduated from college, Helen ran

MacMurray College's riding department in Jacksonville, Illinois. She was twenty-seven when she married horse-trainer Charlie Crabtree. Ten years later they adopted a thirteen year old boy, Redd.

In 1954, Helen and Charlie were hired as instructors at the Rock Creek Riding Club in Louisville, Kentucky. "It was a little old run-down place with only one show horse on the grounds," Helen remembers. Three years after the Crabtrees took it over, nearly all the stalls were filled with show horses. When some of them began to beat world champions, Helen's reputation as a fine horse trainer and coach began to spread.

*Like many horse enthusiasts, Helen continues to ride competitively.*

Although the three Crabtrees were happy at Rock Creek, they had always dreamed of a place of their own. Eventually they bought a forty-three acre farm twenty miles east of Louisville while still working and living at Rock Creek.

It was an incident at the Kentucky State Fair Horse Show that prompted their move. A Rock Creek rider placed second in a class. Instead of accepting the judgment graciously, the girl marched up to the judge and demanded to know why she hadn't won first. Charlie and Helen helplessly watched, unable to control such poor sportsmanship.

During the drive home to Rock Creek, the Crabtrees decided to move. They wanted to start a riding school where they'd be free to teach those who could accept defeat as well as success.

When the Crabtrees first settled into their new home, Helen worried that no one would drive twenty miles from Louisville to take a lesson or to have their horse trained. "But so many horses began to arrive to be boarded and trained," Helen remembers, "the carpenters couldn't even go home because they had to keep adding more stalls."

In time the training school became so large they needed more room. Helen and Charlie began to buy surrounding land, and today Crabtree Farms consists of 204 acres. It has two complete training stables, one run by Redd, the other by Helen and Charlie.

One of the first women horse trainers in the

business, Helen owes much of her success to her parents. Even fifty years ago, when women didn't train horses, they encouraged her to be a pioneer in her chosen field.

If Helen has been discriminated against because of being a woman, it has been mostly in the show ring. Although she is a prize-winning rider, she says, "If I went after the big five-gaited stake in the Grand World Championships at the Kentucky State Fair, I doubt whether the male judges would let me win."

Besides riding competitively, Helen participates in other facets of the horseback riding sport. She teaches even though she herself never had a riding lesson. She judges in horse shows. She also lectures and writes on the subject. Her book, *Saddle Seat Equitation,* is popular with beginners and experts alike.

Helen is well known for selecting the best horse for a particular rider. She will team up a tall, slender girl with a large, graceful horse, or she might combine a

*In the instruction booth, Helen emphatically points out to her students that learning by observation is as important as the actual practice.*

spirited little mare with a small, vivacious rider. The hallmark of the "Crabtree Look" is a perfectly groomed, well-matched horse and rider who give a lively performance.

Once concerned that no one would drive twenty miles for a riding lesson, Helen has taught people from as far away as South Africa and Canada. Crabtree Farms has become a world famous breeding and training center for American Saddle horses and as renowned for coaching riders.

Helen had received many honors for her accomplishments. In 1965, she became the first American Saddle horse trainer to be voted "Woman of the Year" by the American Horse Show Association. More recently, she was presented with a special award at the American Royal Horse Show, one of the three most important shows in the country.

The words engraved upon her trophy sum up her contribution to the field of equitation. They read:
"In appreciation to Helen Crabtree,
great horsewoman, great teacher,
great lady."

## ABOUT THE AUTHOR

**Flora Golden** grew up in Southern California where her youthful equestrian talents were encouraged. She studied English and Sociology at the University of California and presently lives in Los Angeles with her two young daughters, Karen and Elizabeth and their Cocker Spaniel, Randolph. She is the author of two fiction books for children.